FIERY W

Robyn Rowland has written three books of poetry and three academic books. She is widely published in Australia and overseas, in Ireland, Canada, U.S., Japan and New Zealand. Most recently, she was the guest poet at the University of Coimbra, Portugal, where she read in the Teatro Academico de Gil Vicente. In Ireland, she has been guest at the Listowel Writer's Week, read at the Australian Embassy in Dublin and the Yeats Society in Sligo, and conducted workshops in the Connemara. She returns to Ireland in 2001, with assistance from Arts Victoria, for the Australian Arts and Culture Festival, Dublin and for the Scriobh in Sligo. Her readings are described as 'exquisite, moving, inspirational.'

She left academic life in 1996. Before that, as Professor Rowland, she was Foundation Head of the School of Social Inquiry and Founding Director of the Australian Women's Research Centre at Deakin University. She has addressed Trinity College Dublin, the House of Lords London, and has been consulted by governments and agencies around the world for her work in the critique of reproductive technology and genetic engineering. She has delivered hundreds of public addresses and conference papers; conducted interviews and debates on radio, television, and in the print media. In the 1996 Honours List she was made an Officer of the Order of Australia by the Governor General for her contribution to Women's Health and Higher Education.

Published by
Five Islands Press Pty Ltd,
PO Box U34
Wollongong University 2500
FAX 02 4272 7392
email kpretty@uow.edu.au

Cover illustration/photo: Susan Barlow Clifton
Cover design: Jiri Tibor Novak

National Library of Australia
Cataloguing-in-Publication Entry
Rowland, Robyn 1952–
        Fiery waters
        ISBN 0 86418 735 1
        1. Title
A821.3

Australia Council
for the Arts

This project has been assisted by the Commonwealth Government through the Literature Fund of the Australia Council, the Federal Government's arts funding and advisory body.

To dear Mary,

FIERY WATERS

Robyn Rowland

with thanks for your wonderful work, & for the great times shared,

love + best wishes,

Robyn
Dec 2001

Five Islands Press

Acknowledgements

Poems in this collection have been published in the following journals, sometimes with slight re-writing: *Cafe Review* (US), *Island Magazine, Jones Av.* (Canada), *Luna, Overland, Poetry Australia, Poetry Ireland Review, Quadrant, Syllable, The Bulletin, The Worcester Review* (US), *Yomimono* (Japan), *Westerly.*

Poems have also been published in the following newspapers: *The Sydney Morning Herald, The West Australian, The Age, The Australian.*

Anthologies carrying poems printed here include:
Radically Speaking ed. Diane Bell and Renate Klein (Spinifex Press, 1996)
Poetry Involves ed. Denise Scott (Heinemann, 1988, UK 1989)
Up from Below: Poems of the 1980's. An Australian Women's Anthology eds. Irene Coates, Nancy Corbett, Barbara Petrie (Redress Press, 1987)
Poems Selected from the Australian's 20th Anniversary Competition eds. Judith Rodriguez and Andrew Taylor (Angus and Robertson, 1985)
The Australian Bedside Book. A Selection of Writings from the Australian Literary Supplement Ed. Geoffrey Dutton (MacMillan, 1987)

"The Ache" won the Canning Literary Award, Western Australia.

Other Books by Robyn Rowland

Poetry

Filigree in Blood. Longman Cheshire, Melbourne, 1982

Perverse Serenity. Heinemann Australia, 1990; Spinifex Press,
Australia 1992

Other books

Living Laboratories. Women and reproductive technology. Pan
MacMillan. Australia, 1992; Lime tree, U. K. and
Canada; Indiana University Press U. S. 1993; and
Cedar Press, U. K. 1993

*Woman Herself. A transdisciplinary perspective on women's
identity.* Oxford University Press. Melbourne, 1988

*Women who do and women who don't, join the women's
movement,* editor, Routledge and Kegan Paul, London
and New York, 1984.

For Ennis and Tully
    with love beyond measure:

may you always write your own lines
and may we continue to throw light
across each other's paths.

Contents

Life in the flesh

Tangled there

Time-travelling

Bevelled edges

Peopled place

The Great Way is not difficult ...
... for those who do not cling to their preferences ...

Life in the flesh

Hot Art

It begins with your breath.
It begins with your velvet mouth.
Everything does.

Carefully you feed it to the
lick of fire
just molten enough
for persuasion into shape.
Glass, that never knew itself soft,
surprised
at its own moment of flow
finds in itself the flower
arching its back
while your fingers tease along
the stem
dropping the head almost casually
from your hand,
sensing the point when its softening
might hesitate, stop
to cool into glass again.
You know this flower well:
its erect petals
the bud of its stamen
gently pulled into life.

You live among things
you have blown into being.
Beside the flowers, pocked lava seems
to have bubbled into vases,
peacock colours swirl and glide
into balls you can cup
cold yet sensuous in the palm.
Purple, jade and cobalt blue
surge through vessels and goblets
as if you had with your urgent breath
blown all colour from you
leaving only the fire
in your Titian hair,

that ivory skin with its gingery heat
dusted in the coppery autumnal fur of you,
your russet smile
and still, blue blue eyes.

it seems like art,
but of course -
'everything is technique'.

Just a night I remember
we went drumming
at Tyagarah Lakes
on a dark moon
that slipped between
the ordinary and not.
Candles circle the lake
glossy onyx under a sky of pitch,
above you a crown of stars
in a diamond sky
thrown there by Ariadne
carelessly passing by.
We swim warmly naked
in the tea-tree water black,
and the flight of flame seems to spread like
phosphorous across the jet ripples.
Your wet curls
mimic the wheels of after-light
scratched by fire-sticks
into the soft solid dark
as she twirls them
dancing young and naked behind you
on the bank.

There is a lusciousness about this light and dark
that breathes along our skin.
Submerged,
bodies sleek, wet and open,
caressed by the weed,
we are tangled and twined into each other
rhythmic with the drums.

it seems like love,
but of course -
'everything is technique'.

Everywhere the small fine movements of your hands:
drums, glass, sex,
the play of delicate and strong
soft and hard
close and distant,
as full of contradictions and impossibilities
as liquid glass.

Nothing can be given to you.
You tell me you are complete,
without need.
You mistrust words
chiding me for them
scorning them as tarnished and rusted.
But you use them well
to probe, to manoeuvre,
creating only what you want to hear.

That belief in living now,
in being in the moment,
understanding temporality and impermanence,
you use now as seduction:
the slippery words of one escaping intimacy.
Solitary heroes can lose their freedom to the story.
Only connection
measures the valuable boundaries of solitude.
You gauge too much
the length of your own shadow.
Broad and deep, it smothers the breath of love.

I know why the glass finds again
its crystal hardness -
in spite of all your heat.

Young Men

The bodies of young men are firm and
brown all over, silky skinned they
smooth move like dolphins rolling
fluidic in the fluttering slip of sheet.

The eyes of young men are brown flecked hazel
when shirts the colour of new shoots in the apple tree
or the very green of apples themselves
float languid across their chests.

The hearts of young men are patient and calm
not furtive or selfish as the middle aged tell us,
they share, they say 'wait for me to help
I'm here and not hurrying away,
with me the job takes half the time and is half as heavy'.

The hands of young men are slow in loving
they have no sense of time hurrying us on
they do not hear the creaking tread of hours
along the hallway.
Their bodies have no need to rush
revelling in the flesh of women, wave on wave on wave
winding, twining their loving selves long into night into day.

The hearts of young men have been hurt,
they are not saved from pain by being young,
but have learned already loss and grief.
They too fear its sting
its long graze, deep spike,
leaving a dull ache long after the wound has healed.

The lives of young men have been touched by death
they know the souls of those drowned in cars in
the Brisbane River, of those with broken necks when
mistakes of judgement threw the bike too high, too wide,
too skewed it slewed straight into the winged claws of death.

The farewell of young men is sweet with kindness,
tender in parting, they look for friendship
after the body has cooled
and what remains is memory, the journey shared
that wandered back past the years to the wildness inside,
the girl, momentarily forgotten in the
weary tug and push of midlife routine.

Young men are not yet touched by age -
that's all.

Barbed Wire Love

Some people live for years like that:
fingering their dreams like the green nape of buds
swollen but unable to burst,
the crimson scent of soft petals trapped within.

Some people live with the presence
that exits the room during mid-sentence
leaving a wall of silence opaque enough
to make them invisible, even to themselves.

Some people live a life of longing,
too often yearning towards comfort withheld
too often facing a turned back in bed,
always locked into the moat, neither castle
nor green disappearing fields opening to them.

Some people live with the blanket grey
of humourless joyless politics or a
stony striving ambition hardening like concrete,
or merely the monstrous out of control 'I'
suffocating 'You'.

Some people call this love.
Others wither,
dry flower heads on the hydrangea,
russet grass on the compost.
Some people live for years like this.

Vacating lover

Somewhere in the middle,
body firmly fixed in me,
he leaves.
Smouldering eyes smother the flame,
its heat clamorous as bells
warning, ringing in
a crucial torpor of the heart.
I watch habitual technique take over,
the man inside rising ghost-like,
moving off somewhere safe,
escaping the risk of endearment,
avoiding connection that could be too close
or too warm, or too tempting to stay.
I watch him go -
after the perfect cresting orgasm,
after the dressing and the warm goodbye -
instinctively I rush to change the sheets
shower, scrub, exfoliate
that sense of contamination
making love to a human shell
begets.

After your visit

Everything smells of you
twining you slowly into the air.
The bed is still crushed with the
sunlit oil of your skin and
golden spray of your loving.
The turn of your body in sleep
slides still between the sheets.
Even my sarong
you wrapped
tautly round your haunches
damp from the shower,
carries the scent of honey you
let slip languid into your tea this morning.

Space that brimmed with you
holds the shape of your hot form,
shimmering now and wandering the hall
lonely for you,
trailing like an after-image
memories in detail fine as dew droplets
casually caught by a partnership
of spiders web
and the orbed orange of the rising
sea-shrouded sun.

The house is drenched with you.
It will not give you up,
salvage my solitude,
restore the regular pattern of my evenings.
Silence finds me still
detached from impulse to move
listening to the birds settle into the night,
each second beat of my heart gone lost.

Is it that you
were always
a moment only?

Sex

When we were young we thought it belonged to us.
But we were so often fidgety with anxiety,
and that vulnerable self-conscious pain
over our feared unlovely bodies,
we grappled with haste for resolution of any kind.
We had no idea how enviable,
how tantalising,
how voluptuous exciting to touch
with all our unspent tautness of skin,
we were.
We never knew.

In middle age it begins not to matter -
the shape of the body, the softer more malleable flesh.
We know other things.
Now tenderness swells in the air like
the scent of wisteria
clinging along skin on soft Greek nights,
and the best music comes with silence and space.
Just delicate fingertips on the thigh loosens,
just lips whispering hot over the nipple shivers,
moistening the palpable urgency of
waiting and stillness.
Hunger glides into the dark holding back.
In that pause lies the secret of torrents,
of dams bursting rivers across their banks,
while up in the hills fires burn their incendiary caress
toward the open gasping throat

It is the flesh made breath,
the long groan of gratitude deep from in the belly
almost weeping from touch,
the bud of desire broken open
its colour ablaze, the reckless taste of its perfume
wild fresia among the grasses
tonguing its amber
and everywhere dew wet and heavy and the sun rising now and sleep
will come

Tangled there

Close
for Ennis

Disbelief.
I watch you sleep.
Not possible for a mouth
to be so small and perfect pink;
fingers so translucent fragile.
The newness of you fills the house
with a scent so nuzzling in
I know it to be settling into my cells
for a lifetime.

There is not love like this anywhere.
Though the cord is cut
it still binds us through air
twirling in tendrils
round our mutual longings,
winging its way into the years ahead
when the struggle of letting go
becomes more bitter and persistent.

Fear comes.
Not that I nearly lost you.
No.
It was my blood spilling along the floor
unstoppable it seemed,
the great torrent of it like love,
rich, red and unbroken.

Desperate faces rushed about
dripping words like 'failure', 'heart', 'kidneys'
annotating the staccato
of your first cries
grappling with my breast
blind and unknowing.
We clung to each other.
I clung to life.

Now, a week later,
I tremble over you
just to hear your breathing,
the moment
of that breath,
urging it to be audible,
to repeat over and over
and for my ear to stop hearing
the silent pauses between
as if they crash aloud where no pause is.
You are the gift of my mother's dying,
remembered this moment by your cot,
filling me with a longing unable
to know its own boundaries,
my hands reaching for her
in the great night of her absence.

And fear.
You were nearly motherless,
and so soon.
How can it be so easy to lose a mother.
She whose body
still holds your torso warm and tight
while your face feels the first light
and hardens fluid into flesh
shocked into your first awakening.
She who knows you longest
at her death
though rarely best;
she who stands at your cot
knowing she will always count your breaths
watching thought-free longings
beat in your transparent mind.

Mutuality

for Anna

Woven in the constancy of waves
stars confirm
this time of silence shared
in the deep peace of dark.
Friends together
sit
blinded by night
wordless
within the red and white scent
of geraniums.

Separation

Drab overcast shades of winter
insinuate the days like damp
saturating the old foundations
of a once sturdy house.
Yesterday, today, tomorrow
and after that tomorrow,
their pewter dull sameness erases
memory of rainbows, of lips, of sweet pink blossom.
Everything aches.
Such a strange pain,
loss,
so unique,
so common.
Within the ordinariness of groceries, nappies,
the routine harshness of the working day,
the animal heart howls wounded
searching for the screaming place of the soul -
isn't it here, isn't it there?
who cares, who cares.

Then into the open sky between the broken rain,
four Crimson Rosellas
a shock of scarlet in their deep sea blue,
aflame
in the naked apricot tree,
singing,
god only knows about what -
maybe the spare apples
still hanging from the apple tree they gorged on;
maybe that the cat found outdoors too cold;
maybe just that there is
today
and tomorrow
and tomorrow ...

Against constraint

Wanting to be wild again
wind shreds itself
through the Pin Oak
pieces of it jagged
as papery leaves in frenzy
spiral raggedly down
brownly to the dark earth.

Creek, fat and crazy
throws itself toward the sea,
pelts through broken banks,
serrates its tongue
along the rocky bed
where broken cars rust
to the autumn colours, and blood.

Fall, Fall,
everything is falling.
Only the sky remains
blank blue and placid
its stupidity blind
to the blocking and
unblocking of life.

Unbirthday
August 13

This is the day,
this one;
the day your newborn blue eyes
round with wonder at lightness,
at being flesh touched by such a fragile thing as air,
no longer held but free
to begin your unknown journey,
would have searched for me
as you nuzzled my breast.

It was right.
not to make you live
fatherless, perhaps motherless
if cancer had hardened its grip.
Separate, different,
alone among your brothers,
born into brokenness and from another seed,
your father only a memory
flicking his long blond hair
across his shoulders as he strode away
unburdened,
his honeyed love, flimsy memory.

That day of decision
I found the Victorian mourning broach
with its rising sun's slanting rays
across a bird flying above fields of wheat
hidden in the dim reaches of an antique shop.
Carefully twined in its back
his hair and mine lay twisted to remind me
I cared for you too briefly
before by mine own hand
I set you free of us
to search again
for more certain beginning.

What remains
is the memory of rose petals tumbling
pink and red from our hands
into the creek,
your father making love to me
after our ritual to release your soul,
the feeling of your leaving
during the careful
caring scraping of my womb.

I write this only to tell you
that the pain of your passing
does not go unmarked.
The square of earth
beneath the rose tree
so carefully and sharply dug
by him
remains clearly drawn
as if the earth itself, like I,
contains the scar of your leaving.

I grieve for you
as only foolish humans can:
the imagined one
loved, wanted, given up before birth -
sent to me before cancer came,
twisting me to face
the very Being of soul;
to begin the great lessons
of letting go.

Only that I long to hold you close now
and smell your sweetness,
feel your small head soft against my shoulder,
brands my too-hard decision
with its no-choice name.

Erasing

I have moved the asparagus fern
right out in fact
right out
into the garden.
Ten years it has been inside with me,
leaning from the bay window ledge
brushing a breast naked
when I rose from bed,
feathery like breath,
arousing like the pulse of words,
just leaving you tingling for more,
a richer caress or one that's flesh.
It stirred up sense; spoke of other times.
Its been with me a long time.
It became too familiar.

Now there's a young thing
with no history,
no long frond stroke.
It leaves me alone, silent.

Between air and wing
for my brother

1   Thick glass
throws transparent trees
into the room.
I see them out there;
in the window's face;
even in the glass table-top.
That gum
that hangs into our lives,
through cooking, eating, sleeping,
soaks up the colour of night
even before the sky itself.

From here the magpie had soared
with its mate,
relentless in its need
for current, upsurge, drift.
My hand still tingles
with the soft death of it
as I lifted it from the road:
all feathery and fragile bone
as if the flight were part of it still;
as if flight were *in* the bird
instead of some strange conspiracy
between air and wing.

2   Metal bodies at the wreckers
are bent back
like pages in an old book
some careless reader
stuffed into the stacks.
In the heat that frays away control,
she takes photos of her brother's car:
all angles, all ways,
trying to spread it out flat
like a map
to read
who wrenched the wheel, who missed the brakes.

3   Behind the showcase lid
in antique shops,
beside amber beads
and dulled engagements rings,
the pocket watches lie
marooned in mothy velvet.
Derelicts,
they pledge unfading fortunes,
'H.H.K. 1922,
with love, forever,'
the hand long-gone
that held its tick in close.

4   And then there is you
somewhere,
rattling between co-ordinates,
your blond hair and mezzarine eyes,
too naive for the swarthy East,
too suspicious in Europe.
You launch yourself
from park bench to open street,
your face closed hard across
the stamp of vulnerability:
women would think
the softness had gone vagrant.
I ache for each step
that carries your warm wandering heart
no closer to, no further from,
the lost depth in you
that you seek.
If only the sinew
and clumped muscle of you
could swiftly reach it;
winged, mercurial,
could speed you to it.
Instead, somnambulist, you rove across the map,
some inner migration
where the thread seems lost.

Afternoon Gale

Struck
in the violence of dreaming
I shock from sleep.
The great gum
shaking with pain, dripping leaves
crowds wetly to the glass.
Dusk drags me out
into the wind;
into the blackness of its shout
where streetlights
have somehow lost themselves.
Weed-green sea
breaks into blue pewter;
spume is wrenched back
opening itself
its white crust pure
in the clearness of fading light.
Sea-grapes pop under foot.
My face is prickly-stripped
by battering salt and sand,
cut back to phosphorous core,
the passion of clean bone;
or that stone
so smooth and naked on the sand.

Connections

Slicing the avocado
from pear tip cleanly round,
halves dropping open
softly in each palm
the knotted velvet of itself
brown inside,
stuns me silent, brimming.
It is the pure clearness
of soft lemony limey flesh;
its moment of exactness
as it falls away;
and my hands, acting out
some repetoire of movement
memorised unknown to me.

The hands of my father
are gifted with surety
dividing up avocado,
or cutting sapphires so they dazzle blue.
Their life is in the pleasure of precision
seduced by the fascination of reshaping,
driven by the need to delve
as he is meticulous to know
not just the birds,
but their names,
the intimate detail of their flight.

My fingers fiddle unconscious at my throat
for the women's symbol he made.
I see him bending secretive
to his workbench late at night,
melting a two bob piece to cast the sign.
Its bulk is squashed to a tiny cross
striking out from a silver circle,
in which, brilliant as an eye,
faceted by the slightest movements of his wrist,
amethyst blazes purple protest.

I finger the stone,
touch the creamy fruit
with its rock-like cone,
wonder at this taste for delicacy,
and I am moved, simply,
by loving him.

The Ache
for Peter A

You are ill again
or in retreat,
your body curled
in that crusted beaten shell
the stopper tight
against intruding life.
I live once more
by the sea that glowers
as sunset breathes its apricot bloom
across the headland,
blowing the waves oblique toward the rocks,
no symmetry in its cockeyed grace.

Once,
you kneaded bread in the kitchen,
pounding it,
the smooth flesh
elastic and rich with grain.
Tall cliffs,
and the old miner's house
hung like a wish on the edge,
its verandah open
where we thumped crazy dances.
Driftwood spat salt
flames against the dark scarp,
your hair thick as steel, and grey:
a violet scarf,
defiant, dapper.

Which part of you suffers;
Lebanese or Irish,
tale-teller or shearer?
You turn your back
mollusc-black,
against the blue cloth of sea
and its damask-white rim,
shrinking,
even from those sun-bright cliffs.

Early Autumn

Reluctantly
summer leaves the earth;
fierce flare of autumn
burnishes the trees.
Full-bodied foliage
in the Claret Ash
shrinks its dark green heart.
Into this drench of colour
news comes
of your death.

Turning from my day
of galleries and dinner and pleasure,
I stub two white carnations
in the cut-glass vase,
and sit,
deliberately,
to watch them brown
like dying summer.

Today I bought the bark painting 'Woman':
etched skeletal in white
the thin lines of her limbs and tattooed body
protrude among the slubs of bark.
And you, at seventeen, lost to leukaemia.

Full moon again.
The back yard opens up
to that new daylight;
its slow tracing of our paths;
the comfort of its silence
against the raging grief of ocean.
White salt mist
wanders through the garden's silhouette
and rings the moon far out in the clear sky.

A small stem of breath
links us to the morning.

Time-travelling

Time-travelling

Strong arms of a drummer,
reach across two decades between us.
In one hand your generous heart;
the other grips a divining rod you say
will guide us together
toward a future only I can see
already holds the loss of you.

Difficult to refuse but I do.
At twenty six, why weave your life
into my middle-aged wandering
staggering under its load of foolishness,
false steps you already correct so young;
my life scarred, its blush a cracked mosaic,
soon my blue eyes fading, joints aching
when the bitter wind of winter bites
reminding us of seasons
each with its place.
Not enough that it's cyclic;
that winter always turns toward the bloom of spring,
that pink and purple blossoms flower
whatever the month.

You peel back your youth to the old man inside,
journey back
past your marriage at eighteen to your mother's friend;
back to the confusion of childhood:
fearful of being alone with your mother
frightened of losing her love.
Violating all boundaries,
she makes you her lover at four,
til sixteen when she kicks you out, unsure of everything
but her dagger love, corroded trust,
her own hidden hurt twisted into her as a child
by her big brother.

Her denial - the great 'no' of your life -
ricochets down the corridor of your dreams.

Grainy wisdom beyond your years,
you choose joy, courage;
discarded cocoon of your pain drying to dust.
Arguing for the moment, you press me
to leave past and future to march on by.
Old eyes earnest and warm
young face flushed with love,
you come honestly:
not by stealth of night
not by seductions of caring
not by manipulation of need or hope or lust.
So much love here, so much.
I grow into it.

We have been together now
for some long journey with its dark and light,
the path sometimes entangled with bracken,
sometimes burned clean before us.
We have made our own mating so right -
a whip bird call that cannot crack
without the second bird.
I have watched you play hand drums
skin on skin,
the tawny gossamer of your hair flying
while head to heart to hand, you beat sound into shape,
a potter moulding vitality into dead clay.
Your eyes gleam the vibrancy of Tigers Eye
flickering amber -
you are lighthouse to a flame
burning within, illuminate.

We hold ourselves in this closeness
a long moment more,
we two time-travellers.
The prescient mellow glow of you
camouflages the want of years -
could be the burnished glaze of autumn
or the golden haze of summer.
How tangled and unclear
are the colours of seasons.

Just another love poem

This love's not common
where are the words.
This love would bind souls to earth.
This would be wings to carry all pain and suffering away.
This lives in the glorious clarity of colour
spring breaks open,
not too hot, nor carrying the chill of winter.
This love knows its place in wholeness,
buries the past and lives now.
It has its own form and lives its life
between, beside and within.
This love gives of itself not draining us.

Not riddled with anger nor impatience
this love comes vibrating clearly
as a bell on the night air
with the starry sky moon-bright
warm, encompassing and folding us
tight against its beating heart
the blood richly red and surging.

This love laughs at rules
that can't imagine
such fiery truth;
kisses away fear that
so many years between us
might bring the end too soon.
.
This love knows its time and its place
and when to change.
The winds of heaven play with us;
no clutching or clinging can alter the flow.
Only its own dance will determine
the new shape of things to come.
We surrender,
and wait.

This ordinary life

This is not your house.
This is not your family.
Yet you clear the kitchen
while I put my children to bed.
They curl content and small;
smooth cheeks and bath-damp hair.
Today their lives were filled
with hippos and camels and cheetah
and I was gripped by the softness of Zebra stripes,
not harshly black and white as we are always told,
but softly smudged brown and fawn
so perfect even into their manes.

I return to you and the fire is lit,
simply because we like it.
The room has shadows and bright places
the warmth of companionship.
We are tired from the day's work
and nestle into each other,
mimicking the cuddles of kids
to watch a film only you would pick:
'Rosencrantz and Guildenstern are Dead'.
You tell me how Shakespeare did the sound effects for theatres
before he took to writing plays:
the note a percussionist would remember.

Our drums sit ready in the back room
just waiting for touch to live.
Beyond them I know the bougainvillea
riots across the roof,
cerise and shouting its final rush of colour.
Firelight spills across Christmas lilies:
their sweet open scent fills the room.
I breathe it in fully, and the shared stillness sighing.
In this ordinary moment -
all that is needed.

My eyes are wet with it.

Transcience

You read Tarot
turning our future over
in the bungalow
smothered in green bougainvillea
its colour sucked dry.
Voices of children
play hide and seek
among the dead pile
of old tree roots.
The sun warms slightly
as autumnal days do.
I cut the jasmine back
still flowering its small white
crystals of scent.
Wildly it grows and urgent.
It doesn't seem to understand.
Everything comes together
mellow and struggling,
unaware yet of
the barren sleep of winter.

Alone again

Somewhere tonight
you lead the full moon drumming
in an open field,
windswept,
your hair curling around
the currents of wind;
cape flying;
the Welsh chant you wrote
a celebration of your newness.
You ask me not to come.
Impossible to be single
together.
Love strikes its jagged light
into the night sky,
the loss of you howls
at my doors and windows.

Absence has no shape
no solidity;
just vacancy,
just nothing,
no-one there;
quite simple really.
And quiet;
so very quiet.

A stretch of time

I will wake one morning
and you won't be the first thought
on my mind.
I will wake one morning
spread-eagled across the whole wide bed,
not curled on one side
the vacancy throbbing.
I will wake one morning and the dull bleeding
ache of it will be gone
for a moment, then a day, then a month.
I know this.
I watch the plumage of clouds pass across the eggshell
blue dome of sky,
I watch the petals of the roses pink to brown
fall onto the fire's ashes
scattered around their roots.
I watch the steady aging of my skin
and remember yours still smooth
and silky taut.
And I know it.
But for now
you are just gone.
And I miss you.

Holding pattern

Into our grief at separation
comes still the radiance of love
striking open this moment into
the ravelled channels of the soul.
Three months and the heart's constancy
still throbs.

Shared life shards itself.
Pain, reptilian,
slashes its great spiked tail
about in the gut.
The future
formless, without definition
is awash with uneven tides
capricious currents,
no charts or even compass points
to set course by.

But here, now,
we breathe in tenderness.
Our hands know each the map of our flesh
its taste, its scent,
the salty lick of it on the tongue.
Sliding into a wet dawn
we move into a rhythm
so well known it seems one dancer only.
Skin on skin,
beneath,
within skin;
every cell of me is drenched with you.

Urgent, sensual,
a strange excitement grips us
as if it were the first time;
sadness weaves through our kiss
for what may be the last.

And within it
the holding protective,
like coming home
after all the weary travels are done;
crawling frozen into bed
to be wrapped in the other's deep pulse.
Here, where we are known and still loved,
here, where we are loved as we are known,
there is precision,
a kind of flawless fit.

After all
this is complete.

This floating bond

I always knew
this season would take its course.
Breaking the rules,
 we raced along the wet sand
just ahead of the waves.
Lacking youth I was high on joy
my purple skirt flying
enough to carry us both skyward
had we lightness.

Two years weaving in and out:
long enough to have memories
of your skin changing from Celtic pale
with the moving slant of sunlight in summer dawns,
to the burnished glow of it beside
the fire you build this winter, cold now
and coming into dark too soon.

You, whose early life forced you
through a funnel of growth
way beyond the simple counting of the years,
want now to have one more grasp
at being young, even foolish.
Too close this, too deep you whisper,
for one who needs to wander finally
the almost-lost landscape of your youth.
Your gaze turns, ever so slightly
away
as it should;
excitement, eagerness,
thrill in currents as
you walk somehow lightly
into the opening of your life.
Within all the rightness of it
loss runs me through;
sadness winds its red and heavy river
in my veins.

Love does not leave the honest heart.
'We can still hold it tight to us
special in the many forms of caring' you say,
and I wonder at your faith
that this strong bond will hold
when we call it friendship
stripping the flesh from it,
cauterising its multi-veined intimacy.

And I am left floating.
I can still visit the country of the young,
travel in it, even stay for a while,
but I can no longer make my home there.
And I cannot seem to find a place
at the table spread before me
set for middle age.
They will not shuffle to find me space
and the winter browns and
dark lightless wood of it
do not draw me.

This morning
walking on the beach,
I saw a black swan
its neck arching elegant
swimming in the sea
incongruous in the rising sun's
enamelled path,
looking as if this is where
all swans swim,
though you and I know it to be
some passing swanish fancy.
Yet its solitary splendour,
the clarity of its dark sheen
against the light blue sea
made everything right that is.

together, apart, solitary,
everything right that is.

Bevelled edges

Red threads

Her head is a kite in the wind
trailing its screams across the sky,
jagged scarlet streamers tearing
blood from the torn edges of her throat.

The truck bumps across rocks,
skids to avoid her and all the others
running before it, running after it,
feet cut by serrating stones
pocking the tyre tracks
with crimson rain.

He is seven, he is frightened.
He'd hid in the long grass
and watched his sister dragged
from the kitchen doorway,
seen his mother and aunty
hitting with all their strength,
smelt fear just too late
when he came too early back to the house
grabbed by the last man past the door.

Later, herded into rooms with too many beds,
the big whiteness of the man crushing him,
he thinks of his mother
grinding seeds to flour for flat bread:
no, he won't be flour, puffed away with a grunt.
'You little black bugger' he'd said -
bug, he thinks, I'll be a bug
a lady bird, red and black and small;
fly away into the trees of memory
and the sand river, hiding the real water beneath
where he dug like a wallaby to drink -
clever country.
He wishes he could be a bee with a sting in its tail
but red and black he is, blood everywhere.
'You're too small anyway'.
He stayed small.
He thought small was good.

At twelve he ran away from school
where they made him sing about being
young and free.
He started growing:
a foot in three months.
He started hearing other songs
like bees humming in the spring flowers -
he couldn't see them, but he could hear them
and he knew they were there somewhere.
Maybe the humming would make a map
or a song web to catch him and his sister again
and carry them back into the warm kitchen
with his mother singing, not screaming.

He's big now, a man, black like thunder.
He wakes from dreams now
where she's a dragon head
screaming poppy-red flames.
Long time she's been colouring the sky
one way or another,
but it's too long trying,
only her throat remains,
everything else lost.
He's still afraid.
Won't let his kids run free - too strict they say.
'Scarlet rivers', he says,
you don't forget 'scarlet rivers'.
He's still waiting though
for his mother and sister.
He thinks they'll find him one day
if he just holds onto the red threads.

They tell him it's O.K. now -
it was just the times,
and there weren't many anyway
so it's O.K.
Some people trying to make amends now.
He saw the sorry books.
He thought maybe he should sign one.
He's sorry it happened;
he's so sorry.

dreaming real

the night is restless
wind ragged & heaving
like the sobs of women.

I had this dream
woke sweating & wet-faced
ears crammed with weeping.

men are striding stiff-legged
briskly toward spot lit trucks
their arms so full of babies

they dangle from their belts
like scalps or fleshy pelts.
overloaded they hang haphazard

by an arm or leg screaming,
a comic strip where
people beaten never bruise

but these are bleeding, tearing
bundled together like overripe fruit
small fingers reaching, mouths searching

for a breast that links them
to that dark tunnel of love
where light was cold, unnecessary.

trucks rev, boots kick aside
cacophonies of reaching
and in the dusty tracks

women stumble wailing,
this group mainly Asian,
mothers on hopeless parade

stretching out pleading arms
followed by bloated bellies
of children starving for everything,

almost. so many tears
a kind of slippery green saltiness
wells behind them in waves

but it's best you see because
they can't feed them
so warehouses full of boxes

stuffed with children
wait ready to ship them
out to those who can.

turn the page to
Aboriginal women forced
to live out indifferent lives

in the wake of more colonial
swaggering. 'protectors' guard
the safety of the young

wrenching them from the frantic
grasp of mothers to serve
as slaves in the deep whiteness

of cities, to wander bewildered
through their lives searching for any
tangible trace of sister,

brother, of the lungs that keened
to her screaming as she was dragged
kicking into protection,

and in Argentina, Madres de la Plaza
Mayor, mothers of mothers
or pregnant daughters, the

'disappeared', quaint euphemism
for murdered, tortured, rent,
keep silent vigil more pressing

more harrowing than monuments
more 'eternal' than the flame
for the unknown soldier.

and you, my friend, white
gaelic with your soft
skin & shock of Titian hair

not forced, not tortured
but 'for the good of the child'
a daughter relinquished

to save family honour,
one of the army of women
sacrificed for male shame

for you each year the oleander
flowers pink as the crisp cotton
dresses of small girls.

everywhere the empty arms of
silent mothers relinquishing blooms.
the shadows of the heart are long.

The Burying of Hughes
(for Sylvia Plath
Hebden Bridge)

I wasn't there but the story
has it that five women stood
in the grey morning mist of a
Yorkshire fall, the Dales burning,
leaves licking like flames along
the trees' trunks, & in the farms the
animals were stamping & steaming into
the dawn, & the track the women'd come
from a night of poems was full o'mud &
slushing past the wellies, but a sunny
day was promised though the air was chill.

Such a simple act of identity it
was, where the grave lay disattended &
others had been before, laying a
heart of green stones, the women's sign,
tying purple ribbons to a hopeful rose,
but the stone was cheap and grey forced
into erection by discovery that
her body had lain with no name, but
now he had given it three names, though
no decoration caressed it, & 'In
Memory of' had no loving in it.

Anyway, there was this simple act, call
it political, call it artistic, call it
the act women do and redo
to name themselves or take back their
names, though some would call that
desecration, & the hammer did ring out too
loud at each tap & the women did hold
their breath as the postman passed, but
the letters were cheap leading & fell easily, &
the old church hardened its walls in protection &
the tall dark trees fired fierce amidst the grey.

Then silence. For a moment they stood with leaves
clustering & the sun beginning to stir among the graves &
a heavy kind of sigh fell while
they gathered each her letter, & the H
was hard & bent where the chisel
almost broke its back, & the hand that held
it felt the sigh & the chill air warming
into day, & the eye saw the work done
where it says 'In Memory of
Sylvia Plath' - & the faint passing across
the stone of the imprint of 'Hughes' .

And then truth

East Timor, September, 1999

for Tully

Wattle birds sing loquacious spring
in the dark pink flowering gum,
giant that it is,
hanging its huge and laden branches
over everything in the garden.
Trees and plants are bringing forth their goodness,
their purple and white scent tilting the head back
greedy for just a little more in the breeze.

His flushed six year old face
aspark from bike riding under all this petalled richness
finds me stunned and helpless
newspaper falling from my hands
tears streaking their useless track into the moist earth
I dug yesterday.

He sees the photos
he asks 'what is war'?
He says, 'they're not killing the children though
are they mummy. It's just soldiers.'
I tell him yes,
they are killing the children,
the army of our neighbours
whose language he learns at school
uses in the classroom every day
their culture familiar as exciting , full of fried rice and wonderful music.
He says again,
'but not the children and their mothers mummy. Not them.'

'Yes'.

I don't tell him, it's priests and nuns,
babies at their mother's breasts
or floating in the warm waves of the womb,
and small children already afraid
and daddies and grandfathers

trapped and hunted.
I don't tell him they are wiping them out like
his friend hosing the ants off the footpath,
when he cried angrily to stop, not to kill nature
'we don't do that ' he said.
'we don't kill nature'.

I don't tell him because already he is white with shock;
already his world shakes at him,
his grip on all that's right loosens
to encompass the gritty smallness of this truth.
His blue eyes are dark and wet.
'But why do they kill them mummy?':
I am speechless.
'How do they kill them mummy'?:
I am breathless.

My face works its way up into the gum
weeping its pink seed into the coming summer;
I understand the shrill staccato of the wattle birds
more than I understand this.
Calling it evil doesn't help -
the frightening twisted face of human possibility.
Politics aside, commerce aside, power aside,
someone has to wield the machete, pull the trigger.
Someone has to go on the hunt and
find inside themselves some kind of sense of celebration
in what they're doing.
Someone has to live afraid of that in themselves
picking up their own child to swing them laughing high,
making love to their wife.
Can they
explain it
to them.

At bedtime, fearful, he asks to sleep with his brother,
and for me to sing the lullaby where 'thy slumber is blessed'.
He asks me to include not just him and his brother
but 'all the people of the world, even the mean ones'.
For him, less comprehending but more compassionate than I
my dry voice offers it up.

Circus elephants

Small flat slapping ears
you want to lay a cheek against

hides dark-dawn grey and wrinkling
moving restless and rhythmic while

railway tracks and peering eyes
of strangers cage them.

Dying for water, trunks flick hoses
throw hay across their backs

relishing the tickle, trickle
stirring the memories of far spaces free.

Trainer shouts abuse, roughly
brushing them to show-ring cleanness

She backs off, spraying hay skyward
pinch of salt over the shoulder for luck,

but the worn, shrunk tyrant grabs a
hooked metal prod jabbing in hard.

He spikes her to her knees submissive
shouting 'kneel you mole'.

And she cries a dolphin squeal high
pleading, childlike begging relief.

Wincing, I see how colossal she is
how strong, how dark with her one foot

that strums along the chain binding
her other leg, ringing music from bonds.

Just the one great foot, used in times past
to hold umbrellas for the rich, could

crush maggot-small this cruel fleck
thrilling to his prod of power.

If only she knew her strength
if only she felt it, was sure of it.

Instead she cries for water, waits the
whips direction. Chains off, she queues

demurely in line, ready to parade the
ring, doing tricks, dancing for the crowd.

Boat-woman

My body is chained to the bend and roll rhythm
digging all day in the new garden.
Straightening, behind closed eyes
matted couch grass and weed.
Departing sunlight paints the inside leaves of new maples,
flashing like tinsel in a capricious breeze.
Oceans I have seen like this
with sun shot aqua into the arching waves: reef-shallows.

Urgently orchestrating sweetness in my garden,
jasmine, honeysuckle, wallflower, roses;
I want to somehow balance
the bitter truth of her:
hawk-brown skin and almond eyes
raped by Thai pirates at twelve.

Morning news came, again,
of forty women taken from the boat-people again,
and the twenty lucky ones
cast overboard into the path of the oncoming rescue boat:
female buffer zone; twelve years to twenty-four;
all raped in their fifteen minutes aboard.

Her sea is ink, light-less.
Her eyes retreat inwards to search for remedies;
pastilles to burn inside the space that is now her, or
attar of rose-petals.
Her memory dives deep
struggling for greenness and heady perfumed flowers;
rivers like cut glass and apricot light though the ferns.

I have only another hour of light to finish this planting
in hope of mellifluous blooms to come.
They say to plant now in anticipation of spring;
before the soil bitters and mordant weeds germinate.

That last walk   for Rebekah

Carnations I send -
see their crisp dark strength,
smell heady sweetness in their breath,
they are us, we are with you
breath and bone.

At seventeen
all our heads are filled with starlight
walking in early evening
romance at our sides
pulse beating in anticipation of touch or
the taste of kisses,
waiting for seas to lie silken
with moonsheen.
I too have carried the dream
gossamer in my hand,
held it up to the moon
seen its silver promise translucent.

But five men found you
daring to stroll in twilight
self-contained, inner smile on your lips.
No track will ever walk the same.
Even the log-bright light of day
will not still your chills and trembling;
soft flesh that yielded in dreams
wrapped now tight in fierce defense,
broken, wounded, limping after its youth.
That lust for power they hollered into the dusk,
echoes like a great bell celebrating, warning,
clamouring through all our lives night and day.
Uneasiness finds us locking the gate
drawing the blind
and the bell still tolls.

You do now what others cannot.
You stand, shaking
and speak.
You name them
you tell their acts, gagging.
Their kin abuse you
making for the witness stand,
brutal, gutteral ;
they piss on you
second time round.

Over and over we do this:
pick up the needle
thread it
take the silks our skin knows
handed mother to daughter,
sister to sister,
sew ourselves back
till scarred, multicoloured
we uniform ourselves
for maybe one last battle.

When Poseidon raped Medusa
would those vipers have grown so strong
binding her isolation
if she had screamed it to the gods
wept it to the women?
Still,
she turned them to stone
who came near.

In this moment I want to be in those old myths
where vengence from the gods matched the deed.
I want to scream:

Here are the snakes
sting them
watch them twitch their death-dance
bodies hardening to parody flinty souls.

Here is the stone knife-sharp
slice them
see their blood retch clotted black
as the womb's when it holds back hopeful.

Here is the boulder
smash them
see head hair flow, smudge into flesh
eyes stuck piggy-scared under its fall.

Here is the broom
sweep them
bits of broken crystal, dangerous even in slivers
wrap in the smeared pages of your newspaper trial.

I want to say
anger is strong, give it voice:
grunt, root, gore wild-boar sure,
but the words stick.

Mute my anger:
I send you blood-red flowers
bone and breath.

The solitary study of women

Genital mutilation occurs throughout Africa, Europe, South America,
Australia, South East Asia (Leghorn and Parker)

(He) raped and sodomized the fifteen-year-old girl
then cut off her hands saying 'Now you are free'. (Griffin)

Pages flurry my sight:
bent shrieks of girls richochet
sieving soft evening like strobe lights
riddling their hacked future
reverberating ; echoing   on on

Here shaft the body-ripped
screams of girls' nether-lips
sewn together to be torn
by husbands who own them
pleasure and pain
or in childbirth, head struggling
desperate for breath
tearing mother jagged in its first act.
Daughters in their mothers hands
their own gentle touch of pleasure
cut, excised, securing market marriage success.
Fastened, no straying risk.

No arms to hold me, to renew. No stroking fingers
brush the ash of their cadaverous living from my eyes,
or voice soothes with sounds of sweet imperfect dreams.

I miss you in this place.
Where is comfort now;
the slender moment of tenderness.
Alone my night fills with blood.
Rapier voices slice into the corners of dreams.

Prelude: the slaughter of spring

'Some infinitely gentle
infinitely suffering thing' (T.S. Eliot)

Waves crash over-loud,
smashing through locked doors and windows.
I sit
tight
taut
breath reined in
like a fishing-line rock-snagged
that the sea rushes and drags
taunting it
to yield loose to its violence.

Freezing tonight
with a fierce and angry she-moon.
Ice shackles the
Rainbow Warrior
as she labours against its bulk
creaking, striated.
The old converted fishing boat
strains to reach the seals.
Moist-white mothers
slide calm and nescient across the drifts.
mellow after the shiver of birth.

Canada's Spring perverts its purpose.
Any thing club-like and piercing:
spike and pummell through all our floes
long after the spring has ended.
Unrestrained
breath expels its groan
long and rumbling
like the warning of overdue storms

and the seals still scream
into the crimson cold.

Two poems for Eleni

I   On Greek women in the Resistance

We sit here in this catch of time
listen to your words
patching together broken stories
from the smashed remnants of their courage.
Here is a photo of three companions
hanging limp from Mulberry trees
dresses slack, necks askew, in a kind of sad reverie.
One has a bun pinned
at the mirror before breakfast,
before jagged German uniforms
caught them illegally feeding children.
Rags, they drag lifeless now in foliage.

Anti-Nazi, socialist,
hounded in liberation by right-wing rule
they were crushed by a civil war
fuelled by the elocution of British cash.
Shot, hung, tortured to renounce,
clinging to shredded minds and muscle
those who would not sign the Declaration of Repentance
filled Greek island segregated camps.
Stamped 'indeterminate sentence'
dragged to the Dachau of Sounion
the peninsula of Trikeri to perish,
bodies beaten, wrenched in the twisting games
that guards will play with cornered flesh,
they burned their fevered will to ferous strength.

Brutality fed fires of rebirth,
anger turned in them its razor edge against despair.
Each assault, shove, prod,
spurred them to scrape back civilization
hands digging latrines in the rough clay.
Carving hard wood, tormenting leather
they hammered out community,
within the worn spirit of women.

Compelled to hope
stub-fingers scribbled out pain
scraps buried in the olive's sinuous trunk.

Blank walled pages with signs the illiterate
beat themselves against,
under tutoring became words
that jerked and jostled into meaning
a living core of faith
in some free afterlife, after incarceration.

Trikeri today is a picnic spot,
children quarrelling over hiding holes
trampling oblivious the stained earth.
And in Athens, a grandmother stands at the sink
wearied from serving family meals,
turns off her hearing aid
and in the quiet of suds
strains to remember
why it was she struggled so fiercely for life,
bare palms, nails torn to quick
clinging to a future, to change
in that new beginning
after the yawn of the abyss
the long drawing out of the skewer.

Women in Resistance.

II   On parting

Cycling the sea road to meet you
Peloponnese frame our sun,
dropping molten orb in misted blue.
Fluid in softening day,
scent of jasmine and pine skin-wash.
I breathe deep this last gauzy night on Aegina.
This is the end of leonine mornings
bodies stretched languid and browning.
Who will tell me their stories now,
weave tales of adventure and passion

fill my mind with names and faces,
Ariadne, Medea, Helen, Clytemnestra;
and their men
always using love as a kind of currency
their sacrifice as dues
leaving them finally,
wearied from giving,
exiled to arid lands of lovelessness.

We argue with fury
caught briefly in the breath of life
full of poems and retsina.
We play the goddess game
and I give you the gift of eternal memory.
You rail against loss and endings.
But poets, my friend,
are always lonely in the soul.
Too much pain is held there for the line,
too much clamouring sadness.
All the tragedy of the everyday
people carry with them
stored whole with our own longing and lamentation,
is given us, frail vessels,
for making over, for giving back
for finding the small warm spring within
this reservoir of tears.

Sisyphus.

You fly toward me, cycle wheels spinning
in deepening night.
Your bright energy sears the path,
gorse yellow dress flares behind.
Fair hair floods over beaten bronze earrings
burning your own two suns.
I should have gifted you eternal love
instead of memory
isn't that right Eleni,
whose life is lived
in the nerves of your spun-gold skin?

Lost muse

I didn't know what it would do to her.
Thinking the hot parch of desert an
oasis & eyes subdued by mirage &
body torn longing for peace I
laid her down where the stream broke
on rocks & when I closed my blind lids it
still sounded clear like the crystal showers of
Clare Glens & the trees flowered white
into the cloudless sky.

I should have known you'll say
should have known when there were no clouds
that it would never rain again & the
stream would shrivel, blossoms burn
into death & the shade was only shadow & would
fall powdery ash to smother her.

But my sight was gone from the pain of seeing & the
heart had been lost, rent, refound and restitched back
into its cove, but its faint pump barely took
sweet blood into the flesh all new scars & my
arms were dead things right to the spine & a
razor had been sewn into my groin
crippling that long stride which took me wandering
strong across a world of starving souls & sorrow.

So I put her down I thought just to
rest cause she was weary too with
her bright blue eyes fading & her flesh
exhausted into sallow.

And then I must have fallen asleep & wandered
off somnambulist toward the flat plain
of myself where it was not too hot nor too cold &
was peaceful with the sound of birds,
though not their colour, & the scent of salt,
though not the sea, & a shady breeze from the
forests nearby where someone sang me their names.
And I loved to hear them roll off the tongue but

I could not seem to touch them nor reach into
the rings of age submerged & pulsing with their
woody beat & their tales of anguish and waiting.

Anyway I rested and when I went back
again to find her, to swallow her, slip her
revived & panting for me inside again she
had moved from the spot & the place itself
was arid & searing blue & moistless brown.

I searched. For a long time believe me. I could
hear the faint stumble of her tread through the
earth as she looked for me calling. I see
her ragged & beaten draw herself along by
arms muscleless & boney clear, the eyes now
chalky, skin floury & hair a bleach of hay.

She says we may not be able to lie down
in each other again & even the tempest of
colour & light we made may be gone, blanched,
and the baroque indulgence of sense & word
smudged pallid & the bloody rich lines wrung
out into dust. So I hold her wanness
to me tongue to tongue, thigh to thigh, our ragged
pulse waiting for rain & there may be a death here.

Peopled place

Men only

'Cosy Corner', Hepburn Springs

I watch them in restaurants-
couples coming in
from the chill air to the heat.
They sit to settle and eye the menu board,
then, he rises
and leaves to buy the wine.
Always him.

What do they do, all these men going out
for bottles of wine?
Do they breathe the thin night air thankfully
carry themselves whistling and unafraid
into the dark - fortunate men.
Do they chat to the publican
or the numerous others going in and out -
about what - the football, the weather,
their anticipation of the lover who
waits chatting to friends at the next table
in the warm crush of company?

That moment of solitary stride
toward the light of the chardonnay
or the garnet glaze of shiraz,
is hidden and silent and never spoken of.
What do they think and feel
alone in the sky filled with stars
before they burst back
cradling paper bags,
the necessary
proof of purpose?

Breathtaking

Interesting really, that he could do it -
the builder -
break the window

unknown to me
leave the foot-long shard of glass
embedded in the grass

its piercing perfect point upwards
between the tricycle,
the clown-faced ball,

the sand pit strewn with matchbox toys
pine cones, spades
the delicious detritus of play,

next to the child's
blue plastic sandals,
size two.

Exeter dawn

Nothing is
quite so pleasant
as with slight hangover,
after a night serving
dinner and wine to friends,
I stroll out early
in crisp air along
the river, its marshes.
Pass the two women
chattering close and whispery,
sharing their lives
of the night before.
Pass the men . . .
Ah yes, these men
I've never seen them
catch a fish
yet,
but think,
men being as they are,
they must clump
themselves by the river
with tackle
line and silver death,
simply to justify
looking into that stillness
mist rising from a
riverine ice sheet,
white swans beginning their
slice into daylight.

Amsterdam morning

Mist levitates languid from the Heren Canal,
a woman stretching herself naked after love
rising from rustle of sheets to step into dawn.
Sun spins through trees budded with promised flower
as I make for the Rijk museum from my narrow bed
in the long room of my tall and ancient hotel.
She emerges from the full, wide Marriott hotel
pacing me out opposite sides of the street,
two women striding into their sense of crisp air
the sensuous dew-licked spring day,
each aware of power in muscle, calf, thigh,
in fleeting touching smiles
thrusting ourselves toward destinations self-designed.
Breaking our sway of symmetry
she struts with ease into the traffic.
Dress thigh-short pleated heavy from the hip
coloured mauve as hyacinth, belted and ridged with green,
clings and swings in the swanking rhythm of her march.
Her jade bag, fat with the night's takings is
clutched close with pleasure, her smile
mocking the scorn of early work motorists
jammed into idling.

The River Exe

Time is, when alone,
for pausing
dangling the minute.
Hanging
on suspension bridge
my gaze steadies upstream
past two white swans and
the overflowing lock's tassled foam
into still water.
Yellow and white sail, striped, horizontal,
glides across a tumble
of old brick dwellings, boat sheds;
the twisted tackle of a port's past,
which when breeze swings from its lull
becomes again river.
Left bank divides
in vegetable plots
rented out
this country so short of space
lovingly tended today
by short sleeves, bare chests.
Then downstream a
jumbled thicket of
jade and beryl crowds
mauve Mallow flowers,
shouldering their colour
above the baggy
sway of current
disappearing under Water Lens
that closes
granny apple green
the river's sight.
Fleeting instant:
sadness lingers pensile
that I cannot share with you here
my friend
this summer lassitude,
its frond like drift.

Belonging

The road is my twine
gathering it up in the hand
seeking the way back
into comfort
in the tracks where the past has gone.
Embroidery I sewed once
in thin silks stripped from opal
spreads now,
I am stitching myself back into the country,
into the smooth and boneless flesh
of this pencilled line.

While I have been away
trees on the bank
have crept into the Murray,
delicate
have tripped into the deep
their tips tingling with the change.
Seduction, this river,
this stained glass scene
from which the trees press forward,
rising.
Mirror grips their roots.

River and road are threaded
back into the country further,
further in,
where early women pushed
on the dray with their husbands
breaking the cords of Corroboree,
the Rainbow Serpent drained
with the drying waterholes
till its colour was bitumen
and the air round its dying carcass
was sheep.

Women who broke themselves
along the length of the land's spine,
drowned in floods,
desiccated in the sun,
married as a stopper for his loneliness
to save him from madness or drink.
Unable to lance the obdurate crust of him,
she is left month on month
for roundups or droves,
looking out across the vast plains of marriage.
Two of them labouring together
stacking hour on hour, year on year
against their youth
that dried with the billabongs;
a land coughing up bitterness
while they worked it sternly, slowly
into their skin, their lungs, and down
bred into their children:
the mesmerising earth, lizard-hot,
hawk-brown, florid in the heat;
the stumpy scrub that shoots flowers
wild like fire, in spring;
and the green that eludes its naming,
chameleon to our moods.

At Warragul, a watering hole is now picnic grounds,
the Tarago river dribbles creek-like.
How then, sitting in green stillness
bordered by highway,
can I hear bellbirds so clear
and there, behind, the rattle of old chains
as teams roll toward the hills.
Some drift of memory with the place, perhaps,
like the slow cal-um-pa , cal-um-pa
sounds of crossing old bridges now gone,
not rotted but rebuilt because we couldn't believe they'd last.
The sampler fills out, each leaf cross- stitched;
bird and river and road are needled in,
tattooed in the blood.

Team up ahead

Edna Jessop is adamant. She would take a full team of women if she went droving again.

Cattle move slowly.
The rivers of her age
run more surely each year
from neck to breast.
Boss drover at twenty
her eyes have taken on
the grey-green tinge of bush,
searching ahead
away toward that distant spot
that holds night camp
and scent of damp beneath dry clay.

Or further still
toward that team of hers
she sees far out in shadow,
quicksilver, thin of movement
their sure swaying moving among the herd.
Instinct threads them
through the matted trees,
no more strength needed
than every childbed found.
Fever up
feeling with blind hands
moist hope
among the curves and arid spaces
of their land,
they thrust back the scalded bark
of last summers fires
where the breathing green shoot
struggles for its grip.

She shakes her head
to swot away the thought.

Her hand moves along the mane
and that quick dip
before the hard muscle of the neck.
Horse-warm it wrenches at the reins,
and wheels her around...

They are still moving
out of reach along the line of trees.

Ash Wednesday, 1983

This day, fires burned on eight fronts throughout South Australia and
Victoria, killing over seventy people; destroying property and stock.
Among the twelve firefighters who died in Victoria, was Dorothy
Balcombe of the Narre Warren brigade.

I. Sweet country

I   We saw one at Hanging Rock
so I know you would believe it in the Dandenongs.
A kookaburra three feet away hesitating
head of bristle fluff cocked alert to safety.
Thinking this snake too easily vanquished
it beat and beat a chop tail on dirt
till proud, satisfied, it wheeled
across a line of trees into the valley
burnished by collusion of sun
with the relentless rub of wings against the leaves.
Behind, huge rhododendrons white and mauve
sprayed their extravagance across the lawn.
A kind of ache shimmied its way along our limbs.

II   Caroline, we burned along the Great Ocean Road
chipped out of rock by soldiers frenzied to forget,
chained to nightmares and after-war neglect.
Everything was full; the sand ripe- peach;
and the forest conspired in our delinquency
creaking with its weight of birds and foliage
till Lorne appeared like some mediterranean dream
its muddle of hills behind.
Fiery titan, your hair ignited in the sun
ablaze against malachite seas
and we were seals in suits of slippery jade
playful in the buffet and shoot of waves.
Ah, the drawling idleness of basking on a weekday.
Back through Anglesea gazing seaward
we prowled round Rhonda's house
feeling the wood solid against the old chimney,
slab steps scattered with gum flowers.

III   How long will memory grip these images
like birds clinging
to an unburnt branch in a ocean of ash?
Longer than the numbers which rumble over radios
regular as breathing or death rattles in the chest:
numbers for Red Cross; for firestations;
numbers for victim lists, for missing friends, for lost kids.
Memorised now they are ledgered
with libraries in mansions at Mt Macedon,
the first bark hut at Aireys,
our small history we try so desperately to keep,
drifting in flecks along the twists of smoke.

II. Fire

1.   Lorne, Fairhaven, Aireys Inlet.
Torrents of flame tear along the coast
impelled by wind that taunts rage
urging it, inciting it on in bellows,
scalding air, trees, skin,
readying them for the lick of pure flame.
Sucking out life, it gulps and twists
dodging puny hoses hissing to steam in seconds.
Paint lathers on cars and trucks
easy as a child's soap bubbles,
glass melts in yielding desperation.
Minds share the fascination of dancing snakes,
the terror of cornered deer.
Clinched in death, sanity slackens,
his face screams buckling in the heat.
And she, whose flutter of disquiet
had driven her to the highway
cowers under rugs in the back seat,
eyes grained with the wartime disbelief of trenches,
skin flinching as sparks nail the car,
spiking into her sleep to ferment in the nights to come.

ll.   And the people run stumbling in orange fog,
lost in a darkness that breathes
in and out against their throats.
Anglesea beach blackens with them,
groping for children and dogs,
glad for the regular plop of waves
lapping their calves, their silence.
Among this company of strangers
each mind dwells upon that creaking lounge,
cracked vase, the photos and remnants of family
discarded in trunks, stuffed behind wardrobes
kept in a kind of careless pattern for the future.

As one they turn their faces to the hills.
Capricious now, the shindy swoops
firestorm and flaming tidal wave
bursting its over-ripe sunset,
jagging the crest to a caricature of hell.
Crackling tempest of sound
smacks its way down toward the crowd;
fiery tongues detach, gorging out over cliff grass
snaffling at the sky, fusing with passion to the sand,
to hiss and spit in the salt.
War has a patent on sounds:
the whistling bomb of Germany, rotors of Vietnam
shivering the mind long after the fight has ended.
But no battle had prepared them here
for this din
of the whole world burning.

lll.   For Daisey, swimming to consciousness
through the gag of smoke,
it is the plums that break her.
Full and ripe they hang,
dusky skins untouched.
No wind has dropped them,
no shoulder of fire bruised them
in its blundering rush onwards.
Yet on her husband's face,
peeled back like mango,
a kind of puckering, as if for tears.

III. Remains

1.   You went Dorothy,
among other women sprinkled in groups of men,
boots unwieldy, fireproof coat creaking
the helmet shrinking to a band of pain.
Your hands too gripped the nozzle
felt the rip of water surge through the hose,
aimed it, shiny crystal lance at dragon scales,
heart rising high with the spirit of the quest.
When the chance to escape was lost
and you curled, trapped with the men
beneath the truck,
death melting into you,
did you whisper for us Dorothy to be side by side,
to hold one hand soft in ours
the other joined, linked in steel grip on the hilt
wielding it, plunging the blade
till the beast was crazed no more?

II.   He swells in the Burns Unit at Alfred Hospital.
Alone in sterile isolation his skin sings
rasped by the file of flame to stinging voice,
it is grafted, regrafted, swathed in antiseptic cream and plastic.
And like Hiroshima victims
who walked, auto-humans
their hands held out limp in front
nails dripping from fingertips,
the blank-eyed homeless
wander trance-like round rubble
or lean weeping against their hearths
where a chimney alone rises from the earth,
grotesque relics in some pagan ritual of revenge.

IV. Postscript

l.   Ash hangs snowy in the air
as if shaken in those glass balls
where flakes tumble and flutter on the skating girl.
Trees bent hurrying from the blast
are kiln-baked stiff against the slopes,
or near Anglesea, their heads glossy,
still hold the garish colour of flame.
Hills have a two-day stubble
their grubby nudity embarrassing and haunting
like the ribbed bodies of POW camp inmates.
Revelation is over, baptism complete,
life struggles back in a kind of glacial grace.

ll.   Tie-dyed in black
the sand at Ocean Grove draws on its mourning bands.
Mint-green water has paled
drained by the load it drops
returning again and again to despatch
frozen in pitch
the black feather that flashed saffron in flight,
a chunk of charcoal gum the waves failed to smooth,
an ebony rock stunned white beneath,
and the birds, wings still spread
 stunned, forever in flight.
.

lll.   The land restores its veil,
harshness ravelled in its beauty waits in ambush.
resenting our intrusion, fuelling the need to purge, to shake off
the matchbox history of our passing.
It burns in the core of the place
and we know it -
accomplice to our own seduction -
will allow it to draw us into weaving again
the story of our small lives, specks
in the dance of plain, hill, rock and forest -
till desert traps us, flood drowns us, bush reclaims us
verandahs wide to the heat,
tipsy from love of the place
balancing it tightrope taut.

'The Great Way is not difficult...
... for those who do not cling to their preferences...'

Seng-ts'an (?-606)
Chinese Zen Master
Third Founding Teacher of Zen

Lake Conjola

Night slowly darkens the air
swelling it heavy with lightlessness.
Your boys splash and plop, struggling out loud,
unable, unwilling
to stand and listen in the stillness -
they have no need of silence.

But you and I move away;
eclipse their jerky movements
cutting the lake's face,
leave them with the day,
its endless brightness
that seems drained from us,
stolen from our own private shares of energy.
This pitch we move into
this unillumined dimness,
has its own shades.

The greysilk heron in the shallows
silhouettes pointed attention
toward a boat
gliding round the lake's edge
far enough away not to tempt us aboard.
Sharp rocks and sticks underfoot prod
through the thin protection of soles.
The soft misty rain moving over the trees
clings onto skin,
joining us in its tracery of drops
to heron, water, hills.

If death is only like this.
A dark lake
squid ink trees
soft rain merging skin
friendship
and a misty peace.

Again eclipse

Excited chills
round my thighs in the night garden
amongst the quiet snuffling of smaller life.
Picking jasmine in the dark
under a full moon
watching my own shadow, earth's shadow
lay slowly across her
rolling over the white milky skin of her
making with our own exaggerated shade
a soft edge of dark across her
gleaming lustre, veined blue.

Something so entirely sensual
made up of scent, body heat, salty cold air,
licks at me from the play of shadows and light;
something about the white sweet petals showering my hair,
falling into my open mouth as I reach up high for longer tendrils,
sliding down my back beneath the soft hand- woven rug
I brought back from Ireland
wrapped round me as if
it were held there only to be dropped.

Luminous beneath the insubstantial dimness of it all
something like spirit
moves now in the garden,
beneath skin where scars of living whiten with age,
along the stem of breath,
reaching, yearning into the so starry night sky
powdery like mist or even ash,
a trail of shadow, trail of light.
mystery
and the carnal.

It pulls at me, in all the tender places
and damp,
it pulls the great ocean,
and after the passing of our shadow,
its own astonishing light.

Of cabbages and kings

Friends are good –
they tell me – 'do not be afraid'–
afraid alone in my silent house
with my babies asleep
safe – how safe from this –
'do not be afraid.'

It's just a lump.
Just a lump
in my breast,
the breast you held, you cupped
you covered with chocolate one night
when you said you wanted me to go,
licking sweetness from the nipple,
tongue-talking me into staying.
Playing around as lovers do
you took a photo of it
white and round and pink-tipped.
So ironic that you took that particular snap.
I guess you still have it:
you with your anger,
your tossed golden loving
set like an amber shield against me.

Now we are silent and separated.
Your voice honeyed and intimate
weaving its loving sweetness into the silence,
is gone.
It would tell me not to fear
and I would not be afraid.
How love calms.

Now there is myself,
all that I am,
searching for my own stillness
in the long silence of lightless night.
Just me and this lump.
Me and the sound of my children breathing
so sure of tomorrow,
so sure of me in it.
Oh yes, to be not afraid.

Going home
after Apollo Bay Music Festival 1996

Driving slowly along the cliffs
into the secret deep of forest,
with the heavy sweet smell of gum
dawdling drowsy through the window
open to the dusk and misty night,
mingling with the damp scent of my children
slumbering drunk on music,
I know it.

Somewhere in a room
with a large cream machine
they will crush my breasts
between two plastic plates
and ask me to hold my breath,
then forget to tell me to let it go.
Someone in that room
will peer at those photos
and see barely visible
what the tips of my fingers
and the shaking anxiety of my heart
clearly feel.
She will pierce that sinewy tissue
with a needle and it will hurt
a lot,
and I will leave shaken and shaking.
Another someone will ring me later
to tell me it's 'not good'.
and I will force her to clarity.
'Carcinoma' she will whisper;
whisper because she had to do it once before
for my friend, younger than me
then. She's dead now.
It's true:
the earth falls away.

I feel for it now in the dark driving,
my dear white breast with its
small twist of chaos.
Marble smooth but warm,
it holds body memories:
the touching tease of a lover's tongue;
the sucking thirst
of the pink, greedy, grateful
baby mouths of my sons,
two and five.

Their bodies soft with sleep
vibrate now with the echoes of didjerido.
Their dreams brim with determined brass,
precision strings, the throbbing beat of drums;
rhythms varied as the shades that
darkening twilight smudges along the coast below -
the inky land breaking waves
into the raven sea;
the night sky's charcoal wash
ever lightening with stars
as the clouds grey-fade themselves
into the mystery place where all rain goes.

This winding pitch we follow
slows our bodies still jingling full with jamming
to the measured pace of the cobras dance.
Its weaving is the journey the heart takes
like the constant movement of love,
not wanting or even able to see around
the bends and twists
too far ahead into the tunnelled dark.

We travel this black road together
my two small boys and I,
drenched with the bliss of music
soaked through with love,
silent and in harmony
toward everything sure and unknown.

Two years on
March 1998

There it is again.
I felt it again today.

Walking out of the breast surgeon's rooms
the ardent sun on my skin,
all the colours of impending autumn
fluttering and ready to fall softly
so softly to earth,
the sky deep-sea blue, plumed white;
everything in stark depth
colour, sound and scent.

There isn't a sense in me
not glad to be alive
not brimming full of that
so old-fashioned feeling
gratitude.

I walk past Organic Knots
a chemical-free hairdresser
and think yes, that's me:
organic and knotted into life,
my soul bound into the earth still.

Another year
and I'm still glad to be alive.
Even the heartbreak,
even the lost love,
can't take the shining good fortune
out of that.

This present moment

It began with the word 'lump'.
It began with the hard knowing:
decisions no-one ever really wants to make.
It accompanied me into the theatre;
and walking the tunnel to radiation
where a massive mural lines the wall
full of the colours of spring
and the phases of dark
night carries.
There while disrobing,
lying naked under the great beast
that machine;
my breast carved
now tattooed with borders
like a pink-tipped bulls-eye,
waiting for the zap of rays
they said couldn't burn
my reddening skin.

One year, two, then three, later
I've forgotten it all,
except that journey within,
inside the burning and fear,
turning to face, to leave behind
a lifetime of pain held in the heart
as my measure of being alive.

Camped under the gums
my van door open
I watch the river flowing so swiftly away
feel its very current pulling my skin,
experience no boundaries
within this place without struggle,
not driven by fear or desire
not drowning in loneliness or hunger or
deep sorrow.
Nothing is as beautiful
as this present moment.

My small children run strong and loving
their laughter fluttering among the leaves.
The dry yellow grass sings,
and birds,
that live each hour as an act of faith,
of surrender -
how else would they fly-
loose themselves into air
that cannot be seen or touched,
to be held, uplifted.
And trees know it too -
rain will come.
All they have to do is grow.

Love has come
for the first time out of my wholeness;
and left, peacefully
leaving the heart still full and loving.
Everything moves on,
changes.
My body ages, like everyone else;
it too will have its time.
Nothing remains the same,
even the searching
in which there is no failure, no loss,
always beginning.

Alone and in darkness

'I wish I could show you
when you are lonely or in darkness

The Astonishing Light
of your own Being.'   Hafiz (Sufi poet, Iran 1320-1389)

Travel with me in the dark
when I am fearful and alone.
Travel with me now.

Travel with me in the night
while my mind remembers cancer
writing scripts and stories of death and leaving.

I am tired of poets writing romantically of death
as they often do of love,
so unfamiliar with it, unafraid. So much in charge.

I light candles that somehow comfort.
How soft their light
how bright and warm they burn shortly.

This small altar with Quan Yin
next to the white almost translucent rose
brings close the deep garden quiet after rain.

Shut the mind; its chattering list-making worry.
Forget all friends and lovers lost,
the children sleeping oblivious in their tousled trust.

It can't be learned or given; taught or found;
only known: this stillness that links us
without boundaries, to what is impossible to speak.

Not with rage into those dark waters.
Not with passion or resistance.
Not churning the spume, frantic. Not clinging.

Feeling fear, give it some rightful place.
Feeling calmness shared, and some kind of grace.
Travel with me now like this. Courage sweetly comes.